The Seagull Sartre Library

The Seagull Sartre Library

The Seagull Sartre Library

VOLUME 12

ON AMERICAN FICTION

JEAN-PAUL SARTRE

TRANSLATED BY
CHRIS TURNER

LONDON NEW YORK CALCUTTA

INDIA

This work is published with the support of
Institut français en Inde – Embassy of France in India

✳

Seagull Books, 2021

Originally published in Jean-Paul Sartre,
Situations I © Éditions Gallimard, Paris, 1947

These essays were first published in English translation
by Seagull Books in *Critical Essays* (2010)
English translation © Christ Turner, 2010

ISBN 978 0 8574 2 915 5

British Library Cataloguing-in-Publication Data
A catalogue record for this book is available
from the British Library

Typeset by Seagull Books, Calcutta, India
Printed and bound in the USA by Integrated Books International

CONTENTS

*

SARTORIS BY WILLIAM FAULKNER

Once a certain time has elapsed, good novels come to seem almost like natural phenomena. We forget that they have authors; we accept them like stones or trees, because they are there, because they exist. *Light in August* was a hermetic object of this kind, a mineral substance. We do not accept *Sartoris* and that is what makes it so precious. It is a book in which Faulkner shows himself; we see throughout the evidence of his handiwork, his artifice. I understand now the mainspring of his art: underhandedness. Admittedly, all art is underhanded. A painting lies about perspective. Yet there are paintings that are true and there are *trompe-l'oeil* paintings.

I had accepted the 'man' of *Light in August* uncritically (I thought of him as Faulknerian man, the way one says Dostoevskian or Meredithian man)—that great, divine, godless animal, doomed from birth and bent eagerly on his own destruction; cruel, moral even in murder, and redeemed not by death or in death, but by the last moments before death; and great even in torment and in the most abject humiliations of the flesh. I had not forgotten his lofty, threatening tyrant's face, nor his unseeing eyes. I found him again in *Sartoris*; I recognized the 'gloomy arrogance' of Bayard. And yet I can no longer accept Faulknerian man: he is the stuff of *trompe-l'oeil*. It is all done with lighting. There is a formula, and it consists in not saying, in keeping secret, underhandedly secret—in saying *a little*. We are told, stealthily, that old Bayard is shattered by the unexpected return of his grandson. Stealthily, in a half-sentence that might well pass unnoticed, and which the author hopes will pass *almost* unnoticed. After which, when we are expecting storms, we are instead shown banal little actions, at length and in minute detail. Faulkner isn't unaware of our impatience; he is relying on it, but he goes on with his innocent chatter about insignificant action. There have been other chatterers: the Realists or Dreiser.[1] But Dreiser's descriptions are pedagogical in intent; they have documentary value. Here the actions (putting on boots, climbing a staircase, jumping on a horse) are intended not to depict, but to conceal. We are on the lookout for the

---

1 Theodore Dreiser (1871–1945): perhaps the most prominent novelist of the American 'Naturalist' school. [Trans.]

one that will betray Bayard's distress, but the Sartorises never get carried away; they never betray themselves through actions. Yet these idols, whose actions seem like threatening rituals, also possess consciousness. They speak, they have their own thoughts, they feel emotion. Faulkner knows this. From time to time, he carelessly reveals a consciousness to us. But this is like a conjuror showing us his box when it is empty. What do we see? No more than we could see from the outside: actions. Or we catch off-guard consciousnesses sliding towards sleep. And then, once again, there are actions—tennis, piano-playing, whisky, conversation. And here is what I cannot accept: the entire intention is to persuade us that these consciousnesses are still as empty, still as elusive. Why? Because consciousness is a too-human thing. The Aztec gods do not engage in pleasant little conversations among themselves. But Faulkner knows perfectly well that consciousnesses are not and *cannot* be empty. He knows it well enough to write: '. . . she again held her consciousness submerged deliberately, as you hold a puppy underwater until its struggles cease.'[2]

But what there is *in* this consciousness that needs to be drowned he doesn't tell us. It is not exactly that he wants to hide it from us: he would like us to divine it, because divination makes whatever it touches magical. And the actions begin once again. We would like to say 'Too many actions', the way they said 'too many notes'

2 William Faulkner, *Sartoris* (New York: The New American Library, 1963), p. 133.

to Mozart. Too many words too. Faulkner's volubility, his abstract, haughty, anthropomorphic preacher's style—these too are all optical illusions. The style paints the daily gestures too thickly, weighs them down, overwhelms them with an epic magnificence and sinks them like lead weights. Deliberately so. It is precisely this sickening, solemn monotony, this ritual of the everyday that Faulkner has in his sights; actions are the world of boredom. These rich people, respectable and uneducated, having neither work nor leisure, captive on their own lands and simultaneously masters and slaves to their negroes, are bored; they try to fill up the time with their actions. But this boredom (has Faulkner always managed to differentiate that of his heroes from that of his readers?), is merely an appearance; it is Faulkner's defence against us, and the Sartorises' against themselves. The boredom is the social order; it is the monotonous languor of all that can be seen, heard, touched: Faulkner's landscapes are as bored as his characters. The real drama lies *behind*—behind the boredom, behind the actions, behind the characters' consciousness. Suddenly, from the depths of this drama, the Deed wells up, like a meteorite. A Deed—at last something that *happens*, a message. But Faulkner disappoints us again. He rarely describes Deeds. This is because he comes up against an old problem of novelistic technique and sidesteps it: Deeds are the real stuff of the novel; they are prepared for with care and then, when they occur, they are bare and polished as bronze. They are infinitely simple and slip between our fingers. There is nothing more to be said about them; it is enough, one might say, simply to name them. Faulkner doesn't name them, doesn't speak of them and hence suggests they are unnameable, beyond language. He will show only their results: an old man dead in his chair, a car overturned in the river and two feet sticking out of the water. These still, violent consequences, as solid and compact as the Deed is elusive, appear and display themselves, definitive and inexplicable amid the fine, steady rain of daily actions. Later, these unfathomable instances of violence will change into 'stories': they will be named, explained, recounted. All these people, all these families have their stories. The Sartorises carry the heavy burden of two wars, of two sets of stories: the Civil War, in which old Bayard died, and the 1914 War, in which John Sartoris was killed. The stories appear and disappear, passing from mouth to mouth, lingering on alongside the daily actions. They do not belong entirely to the past, but are, rather, a super-present:

> As usual, old man Falls had brought John Sartoris into the room with him . . . Freed as he was of time and flesh, he was a far more palpable presence than either of the other two old men who sat shouting periodically into one another's deafness.[3]

They make up the poetry of the present and its fatedness: 'fatal immortality and immortal fatality'. It is

---

3 Faulkner, *Sartoris*, p. 1.

with stories that Faulkner's heroes forge their destinies: by way of these fine, carefully polished tales, sometimes embellished by many generations, an unnameable, long-buried Deed signals to other Deeds, charming and attracting them as a sharp point attracts lightning. Such is the insidious power of words and stories; and yet Faulkner doesn't believe in these incantations:

> What had been a hare-brained prank of two heedless and reckless boys wild with their own youth had become a gallant and finely tragical focal point to which the history of the race had been raised . . . by two angels valiantly fallen and strayed, altering the course of human events . . .[4]

He is never entirely taken in. He knows what these tales are worth since he is the one telling them, since he is, like Sherwood Anderson, 'a storyteller and a liar'. Only he dreams of a world in which stories would be believed, where they would really have effects on people: and his novels depict the world he dreams of. We are familiar with the 'technique of disorder' of *The Sound and the Fury* and *Light in August*, those inextricable tangles of past and present. I think I have found the twofold origin of this in *Sartoris*: it is, on the one hand, the irresistible need to tell a tale, to stop the most urgent action in order to bring in a story—this seems to me a characteristic feature

---

4 Faulkner, *Sartoris*, p. 33.

of many lyrical novelists—and, on the other, the semi-sincere, semi-imagined faith in the magical power of stories. But when he writes *Sartoris* he has not yet perfected his technique. He shifts between past and present, between action and stories with a great deal of clumsiness.

Here, then, is the human being Faulkner presents us with, and wants us to accept. He is wholly elusive; one can grasp him neither in his actions, which are a facade, nor in his stories, which are false, nor in his Deeds, which are indescribable flashes of lightning. And yet beyond behaviour and words, beyond empty consciousness, the human being exists: we sense a genuine drama about him, a sort of intelligible quality that explains everything. But what is this quality? A taint of breeding or family flaw, an Adlerian inferiority complex or repressed libido? At times it is one, at times another: it depends on the stories and the characters. Often, Faulkner doesn't tell us. And besides, he isn't much concerned with this: what matters to him is, rather, the *nature* of this new creature, a nature that is, first and foremost, *poetic* and magical, the contradictions of which are manifold, but veiled. Grasped through psychical manifestations, this 'nature' (for what else can we call it?) is part of psychical existence; it is not, in fact, entirely of the order of the unconscious, since it often seems the human beings impelled by it can turn around and contemplate it. On the other hand, it is fixed and changeless, like a curse. Faulkner's heroes carry it with them from birth; it is as stubborn as stone or rock; it is *a thing*. A spirit-thing, a solidified, opaque spirit behind consciousness, shadows whose essence is, nonetheless, light. This is the supreme magical object. Faulkner's creatures are bewitched, a stifling atmosphere of sorcery surrounds them. And this is what I referred to as underhandedness: these bewitchments are not possible. Nor even conceivable. And so Faulkner is at pains not to let us conceive them. But his whole method consists in suggesting them.

Is he entirely underhanded? I don't believe so. Or if he lies, he does so to himself. A curious passage in *Sartoris* provides us with the key to his lies and to his sincerity:

> 'Your Arlens and Sabatinis talk a lot, and nobody ever had more to say and more trouble saying it than old Dreiser.'
>
> 'But they have secrets,' she explained. 'Shakespeare doesn't have any secrets. He tells everything.'
>
> 'I see. Shakespeare had no sense of discrimination and no instinct for reticence. In other words, he wasn't a gentleman,' he suggested.
>
> 'Yes . . . that's what I mean.'
>
> 'And so, to be a gentleman, you must have secrets.'
>
> 'Oh, you make me tired.'

This is an ambiguous and, no doubt, ironic dialogue. Narcissa is not very clever and, besides, Michael

Arlen and Sabatini are bad writers. Yet it seems to me Faulkner reveals much of himself here. If Narcissa is, perhaps, somewhat lacking in literary taste, her instinct is sound when it causes her to opt for Bayard, a man with secrets. Horace Benbow is perhaps right to like Shakespeare, but he is weak and garrulous; he says everything, he is not a man. The men Faulkner likes, the negro in *Light in August*, Bayard Sartoris and the father in *Absolom* have secrets; they remain silent.

I dare say Faulkner's humanism is the only acceptable sort: he hates our well-adjusted, babbling, engineers' minds. But does he not know that his great, dark figures are mere exteriors? Is he fooled by his own art? To him, it would probably not be enough for our secrets to be repressed into the unconscious; he yearns for a total darkness at the heart of consciousness, a total darkness we would ourselves fashion within ourselves. Silence. Silence outside us, silence within—this is the impossible dream of a Puritan ultra-Stoicism. Is he lying to us? What does he do when he is on his own? Does he put up with the endless babbling of his all-too-human consciousness? To have an answer, we should have to know him.

February 1938

＊

ON JOHN DOS PASSOS AND *1919*

A novel is a mirror. Everyone says so. But what is it to *read* a novel? I believe that it is to jump into the mirror. Suddenly, you find yourself through the looking-glass, among people and objects that seem familiar. But this is simply an appearance; in fact we have never seen them before. And the things in our world are now external in their turn and have become mere reflections. You close the book, climb back over the rim of the mirror and re-enter *this* honest-to-goodness world, and you are back with furniture, gardens and people who have nothing to say to you. The mirror that has reconsituted itself behind you reflects them peacefully. After which you would swear that art is a reflection. And the cleverest will go so far as to speak of distorting mirrors. Dos Passos uses this absurd, obstinate illusion very consciously to prick us into revolt. He has done the needful for his novel to appear a mere reflection; he has even donned the dowdy garb of populism. But the fact is that his art is not gratuitous; he has something to prove. Yet consider what a curious enterprise this is: the aim is to show us *this* world, our world. To *show* it only, with no explanation or commentary. No revelations about the police's double dealings, the oil barons' imperialism or the Ku Klux Klan. And no cruel depictions of poverty. Everything he wants to show us is something we have already seen—and seen, as it initially seems, in just the way he wants to make us see it. We immediately recognize the sad abundance of these untragic lives. They are our lives, these thousand adventures sketched out, botched, immediately forgotten, but constantly begun again, which slide by without a trace, without ever connecting with anything, until the day when suddenly one of them, just like all the others, as though out of clumsiness and trickery, sickens a man forever and carelessly throws a machinery out of kilter. It is by depicting—as we ourselves could depict them—these all too well-known phenomena, which everyone normally accepts, that Dos Passos renders them unbearable. He infuriates those who have never been infuriated before, he frightens those who are frightened of nothing. Has there not perhaps been some sleight of hand here? I look around me and see people, cities, ships, warfare. But they aren't the real thing: they are discreetly suspect and sinister, as in nightmares. My indignation against that world also seems suspect. It merely *resembles* that other indignation, the indignation a little story in the newspaper can arouse—and it does so rather remotely. I am on the other side of the mirror.

Dos Passos' hatred, despair and lofty contempt are genuine. But for just that reason, his world is not: it is a creation. I know of none, not even those of Faulkner or Kafka, in which the art is greater or better concealed. I know of none closer to us, more precious, more affecting. This is because he takes his material from our world. And yet there is no world further removed from our own or stranger. Dos Passos has invented only one thing: an art of storytelling. But that is enough to create a whole universe.

We live in time and it is in time that we count. The novel unfolds in the present, the way that life does. Only in appearance is the past preterite the tense of the novel; we have to see it as a present *with aesthetic distance*, a staging device. In a novel, matters are not settled once and for all, for human beings in novels are free. They create themselves before our eyes; our impatience, our ignorance and our expectation are the same as the hero's. By contrast, Fernandez[1] has shown that pure *narrative* is situated in the past. But narrative explains: there, chronological order, the order of life, barely conceals the causal order, the order of the understanding. Events in narrative do not move us; they are located mid-way between fact and law. Dos Passos' time is his own creation: it is neither

---

1 The reference is to Ramon Fernandez (1894– 1944): novelist and literary critic. [Trans.]

novel, nor narrative. It is rather, if you will, historical time. The past tenses are not employed to conform to the rules: the *reality* of Joe's or Eveline's adventures is that they are now past. The whole is narrated as if someone were remembering:

> *The years Dick was little*, he never heard anything about his Dad . . .[2] All Eveline thought about *that winter* was going to the Art Institute . . .[3] They waited two weeks in Vigo while the official quarrelled about their status and they got pretty fed up with it.[4]

The event in a novel is an unnamed presence: you cannot say anything about it because it is unfolding; we can be shown two men looking all around a city for their mistresses, but we are not told that they 'don't find them', because that is not how it is: so long as there is still a street, a cafe or a house to explore, that is not how it is *yet*. With Dos Passos, we begin with the event being named. The die is cast, as in our memories:

> Glen and Joe only got ashore for a few hours and couldn't find Marcelline and Loulou.[5]

---

2 John Dos Passos, '1919', in *U.S.A.* (Harmondsworth: Penguin, 1978), p. 400.

3 Dos Passos, *U.S.A.*, p. 433.

4 Dos Passos, *U.S.A.*, p. 470.

5 Dos Passos, *U.S.A.*, p. 469.

The facts have a clear outline to them; they are just ripe for *thinking about*. But Dos Passos never thinks about them. Not for a moment do we catch the order of causes beneath the order of dates. This is not narrative: it is the jerky unwinding of a raw memory full of holes, which sums up a period of several years in a few words, then lingers languidly over some tiny fact. In this it is just like our real memories, a jumble of frescoes and miniatures. There is no lack of relief, but it is artfully distributed at random. One step further and we would be back at the famous idiot's monologue in *The Sound and the Fury*. But that would still be to intellectualize, to suggest an explanation in terms of the irrational, to hint at a Freudian order behind this disorder. Dos Passos halts himself in time. As a result of which, past facts retain a savour of the present. They remain, in their exile, what they once were for a day, a single day: inexplicable tumults of colour, noise and passion. Each event is a—gleaming, solitary—*thing* that doesn't ensue from any other, but emerges suddenly and adds itself to other things. It is irreducible. For Dos Passos, storytelling is an act of addition. Hence this loose air to his style: 'and . . . and . . . and . . .' The great tumultuous phenomena—war, love, a political movement or a strike—fade and crumble into an infinity of little trifles that one can just place side by side. Here is the Armistice:

> In early November rumours of an armistice
> began to fly around and then suddenly one

afternoon Major Wood ran into the office that Eleanor and Eveline shared and dragged them both away from their desks and kissed them both and shouted, 'At last it's come.' Before she knew it, Eveline found herself kissing Major Moorehouse right on the mouth. The Red Cross office turned into a college dormitory on the night of a football victory: It was the Armistice.

Everybody seemed suddenly to have bottles of cognac and to be singing. *There's a long long trail awinding* or *La Madel-lon pour nous n'est pas sévère.*[6]

These Americans see war the way Fabrice del Dongo saw the battle of Waterloo.[7] And the intention, like the method, is clear when one thinks about it. But one must first close the book and reflect.

Passions and actions are also things. Proust analysed them, connected them to previous states and, as a consequence, rendered them necessary. Dos Passos wants to preserve their *factual* character. We can only say, 'At that time Richard was like this, and at another time he was different.' Love and decisions are great self-contained spheres. At best we can grasp a kind of *match-up* between

---

6 Dos Passos, *U.S.A.*, p. 578. Other editions of this work show that the hyphen in '*La Madel-lon*' is intended by Dos Passos. [Trans.]

7 Fabrice del Dongo is the central character of Stendhal's *La Chartreuse de Parme* (1839). [Trans.]

psychological state and external situation: something like a colour harmony. Perhaps, too, we will suspect that explanations are *possible*. But they seem frivolous and futile, like a spider's web lying on heavy red flowers. Nowhere, however, do we have the sense of novelistic freedom. Rather Dos Passos forces on us the unpleasant impression of an indeterminacy of detail. Acts, emotions and ideas settle suddenly upon a character, make their nests and then fly off, without the character himself having much to do with it. We should not say that he *undergoes* these things; he registers them, and no one can say what law governs their appearance.

Yet they did exist. This lawless past is irremediable. In his storytelling Dos Passos deliberately chose the perspective of history: he wants to make us feel that the die is cast. In *Man's Hope*, Malraux says, more or less, that the tragic thing about death is that it 'transforms life into fate'.[8] From the first lines of his book, Dos Passos has settled into death. All the existences he retraces have closed upon themselves. They are like those Bergsonian memories that float around, after the death of the body, full of shouts and smells and light, in some sort of limbo. We have a constant sense of these vague, humble lives as Destinies. Our own pasts are not like this: there is not one of our past acts whose value and meaning we could

8 André Malraux (1901–76): a French novelist and adventurer and, in his latter years, de Gaulle's minister of culture (1959–69). His novel *L'Espoir*, translated into English as *Man's Hope*, was published in 1937. [Trans.]

not still transform today. But, beneath their violent hues, these fine, gaily coloured objects Dos Passos presents us with have something petrified about them. Their meaning is fixed. Close your eyes and try to remember your own life. Try to remember it like this. You will suffocate. It is this unrelieved suffocation Dos Passos has tried to express. In capitalist society, people do not have lives; they have only destinies. He doesn't say this anywhere, but he implies it everywhere. Discreetly and cautiously, he presses the point till he fills us with a desire to shatter our destinies. We are rebels now and his goal is achieved.

Rebels *behind the mirror*. For this isn't what the this-worldly rebel wants to change. He wants to change the *present* condition of human beings, the condition that evolves day by day. To relate the present in the past tense is to employ artifice, to create a strange and beautiful world, a world as rigid as one of those Mardi-Gras masks that become terrifying when real, live human beings wear them on their faces.

But what are these memories that are unreeled in this way throughout the novel? At first sight, it seems as though they are the memories of the heroes—of Joe, Dick, Daughter and Eveline. And, on more than one occasion, this is true. It is true as a general rule, each time a character is sincere, each time he has a fullness in him of some sort or another:

> When he went off duty he'd walk home
> achingly tired through the strawberry-scented
> early Parisian morning, thinking of the faces
> and the eyes and the sweat-drenched hair
> and the clenched fingers clotted with blood and
> dirt . . .[9]

But often the narrator doesn't coincide entirely with the hero. The hero couldn't precisely have said what he says, but one feels a discreet complicity between the two; the narrator recounts things from outside in the way the hero would like them to have been recounted. Under cover of this complicity, without alerting us to the fact, Dos Passos has us make the transition he was trying for: we suddenly find ourselves inside a horrible memory, and every recollection in it makes us ill at ease. It is a memory in which we lose our bearings, being neither that of the characters nor of the author. It is like a chorus remembering—a sently, yet complicit chorus:

> All the same he got along very well at school
> and the teachers liked him, particularly Miss
> Teazle, the English teacher, because he had nice
> manners and said little things that weren't fresh,
> but that made them laugh. Miss Teazle said he
> showed a real feeling for English composition.
> One Christmas he sent her a little rhyme he

<hr>

9 Dos Passos, *U.S.A.*, p. 509.

made up about the Christ Child and the three Kings and she declared he had a gift.[10]

The narrative becomes a little stilted and everything we are told about the hero assumes the air of solemn, publicity-style information. 'She declared he had a gift.' There is no commentary on the sentence, but it acquires a kind of collective resonance. It is a *declaration.* And indeed, when we would like to know the thoughts of his characters, Dos Passos most often provides us, with respectful objectivity, with their declarations:

> Fred . . . said the last night before they left he was going to tear loose. When they got to the front he might get killed and then what? Dick said he liked talking to the girls but that the whole business was too commercial and turned his stomach. Ed Shuyler, who'd been nicknamed Frenchie and was getting very continental in his ways, said that the street girls were too naïve.[11]

I open *Paris-Soir* and read: 'From our special correspondent: Charlie Chaplin says he has killed off the little tramp.' Now I have it: Dos Passos reports all his characters' words in the style of press statements. They are, as a result, immediately cut off from thought; they are pure words, simple reactions to be registered as

---

10 Dos Passos, *U.S.A.*, p. 401.
11 Dos Passos, *U.S.A.*, p. 420.

such, after the fashion of the behaviourists, from whom Dos Passos takes occasional inspiration. But at the same time utterances assume a social importance: they are sacred, they become maxims. No matter what Dick had in his mind when he pronounced this sentence, thinks the satisfied chorus; all that matters is that it was pronounced. Besides, it came from way beyond him; it didn't form inside him. Even before he spoke, it was a high-sounding, ritualized noise; he merely lent it his power of assertion. It seems there is a celestial store of utterances and commonplaces from which each of us plucks the words appropriate to the situation. And a store of actions too. Dos Passos pretends to present us with actions as pure events, as mere *exteriors*, the free movements of an animal. But this is only a semblance: in relating them he actually adopts the standpoint of a chorus, of public opinion. Every one of Dick or Eleanor's actions is a public manifestation, accompanied by a low murmur of flattery:

> At Chantilly they went through the chateau and fed the big carp in the moat. They ate their lunch in the woods, sitting on rubber cushions. J. W. kept everybody laughing explaining how he hated picnics, asking everybody what it was that got into even the most intelligent women that they were always trying to make people go on picnics. After lunch they drove out to Senlis

to see the houses that the Uhlans had destroyed there in the battle of the Marne.[12]

Isn't this like the account of a veterans' dinner reported in a local newspaper? At the same time as the action dwindles merely to a thin film, we suddenly realize that it *counts*, in the sense both that it commits the characters and is sacred. Sacred for whom? For the vile consciousness of 'everyone', for what Heidegger calls 'das Man'. But who brings this consciousness to life? Who represents it as I read? Why, I do. To understand the words, to give a meaning to the paragraphs, I first have to adopt the point of view of everyone's consciousness. I have to become the obliging chorus. That consciousness exists only through me; without me there would merely be black flecks on white sheets of paper. But at the very moment when I *am* this collective consciousness, I also want to wrench myself away from it, to assume the view-point of the judge—that is to say, to wrench myself away from myself. Hence this shame and unease Dos Passos is so good at imparting to his readers. I am complicit despite myself—though I am not so sure that it is despite myself—creating and rejecting taboos at one and the same time. I am, once again, to my very core—and against myself—revolutionary.

On the other hand, how I hate Dos Passos' people! Their minds are revealed to me for a second, just to show

12 Dos Passos, *U.S.A.*, p. 659.

me that they are living beasts, and then there they are, interminably unfurling their tissue of ritual declarations and sacred acts. Not for them the divide between exterior and interior, between consciousness and the body, but one between the stammerings of an individual, timid, intermittent, inarticulate thinking and the viscous world of collective representations. What a simple procedure this is, and how effective! You have only to relate a life using the techniques of American journalism and life, like Stendhal's '*rameau de Salzbourg*', crystallizes into something social.[13] By the same token, the problem of the transition to 'the typical'—that stumbling block of the social novel—is solved. There is no need to present us with a typical worker, to put together, as Nizan does in *Antoine Bloyé*, an existence that is the precise average of thousands of existences. Dos Passos can devote all his attention to portraying the singularity of a life. Each of his characters is unique; what happens to them could happen only to them. And what matter, since social life has marked them more deeply than any particular circumstance could, since *they are* that social life? Beyond the chance workings of destiny and the contingency of details, we glimpse in this way an order more flexible than Zola's physiological necessity or Proust's psychological mechanism. It is a gentle, wheedling form of

---

13 Sartre is referring to the branches which the miners at Hallein near Salzburg throw down into the abandoned depths of the salt mine in winter. These are recovered two or three months later covered in sparkling crystals. [Trans.]

constraint that seems to let go of its victims, only to take hold of them again later without their suspecting it. It is, in short, a statistical determinism. They live as they are able, these people submerged in their own lives; they pursue their various struggles and what happens to them wasn't determined beforehand. And yet neither their crimes, their efforts nor their worst acts of violence can disrupt the regularity of births, marriages and suicides. The pressure a gas exerts on the walls of its containing vessel doesn't depend on the individual history of the molecules that make it up.

We are still on the other side of the mirror. Yesterday you saw your best friend and told him of your passionate hatred of war. Now try to tell yourself that story in the style of Dos Passos. 'And they ordered two beers and said that war was appalling. Paul stated he'd rather do anything than fight and John said he concurred and both were moved and said they were happy to agree. As he was going home, Paul decided to see more of John.' You will immediately hate yourself. But it won't take you long to see that you *can't* speak of yourself in this tone. However insincere you might have been, at least you lived out your insincerity; you played it out on your own, you extended its existence at every moment in a process of continued creation. And even if you let yourself be dragged down into collective representations, you had first to live these out as an individual abdication. We are neither mechanisms nor possessed souls, but something worse: we are free. Entirely *outside* or entirely *inside*. Dos Passos' human is a hybrid, internal-external creature. We are with him and in him. We live with his vacillating individual consciousness and, suddenly, it falters, weakens and flows off into the collective consciousness. We follow him and suddenly, here we are, outside, without having noticed it. This is the creature beyond the looking-glass—strange, contemptible and fascinating. Dos Passos knows how to achieve some marvellous effects with this perpetual slippage. I know of nothing more striking than the death of Joe:

> Joe laid out a couple of frogs and was backing off towards the door, when he saw in the mirror that a big guy in a blouse was bringing down a bottle on his head held with both hands. He tried to swing around but he didn't have time. The bottle crashed his skull and he was out.[14]

We are inside, with him, until the impact of the bottle on his head. Immediately afterwards, we are outside, with the chorus: '. . . and he was out.' Nothing conveys the sense of annihilation more clearly. And every page you turn after that, speaking of other minds and a world that carries on without Joe, is like a spadeful of earth on his corpse. But this is a behind-the-looking-glass death. What we apprehend is, in fact, merely the fine *semblance* of nothingness. True nothingness can neither be felt nor

---

14 Dos Passos, *U.S.A.*, p. 238.

thought. Of our real deaths neither we nor anyone after us will ever have anything to say.

Dos Passos' world, like Faulkner's, Kafka's or Stendhal's, is impossible, because it is contradictory. But therein lies its beauty. Beauty is a veiled contradiction. I regard Dos Passos as the greatest writer of our time.

August 1938

＊

DESPAIR BY VLADIMIR NABOKOV

One day in Prague Hermann Karlovich comes face to face with a tramp who resembles him like a brother. From that moment on, he is obsessed with the memory of this extraordinary resemblance and the growing temptation to *make use of it.* He seems to feel duty-bound not to let this marvel pass for a mere natural monstrosity and needs to appropriate it in some way. He feels, in a sense, the dizzying impact of such artistic perfection. You will have already guessed that he ends up killing his double and passing himself off as the dead man. Another perfect crime, you will say. True, but this is a crime of a special kind because the resemblance on which it is based may well be an illusion. In the end, when the murder has been carried out, Hermann Karlovich is not entirely sure he hasn't made a mistake. Perhaps he was wrong; perhaps what he had seen was just one of those phantom similarities that we notice, on days when we are tired, in the faces of passers-by. So the crime is undermined from within, as also is the novel.

It seems to me that this zeal in self-criticism and self-destruction is rather characteristic of Mr Nabokov's manner. He is an author with a great deal of talent, but he is the son of old parents. I am ascribing blame here only to his spiritual parents, particularly Dostoevsky. Even more than he resembles his double Felix, Nabokov's hero resembles the characters of *The Raw Youth*, 'The Eternal Husband' or *Notes from Underground*, those stiff, clever obsessives, always worthy and always humiliated, who wrestle in the inferno of reason, are contemptuous of everything and are continually doing their utmost to justify themselves, and who offer a glimpse, through the holes in their proud, faked confessions, of their hopeless bewilderment.

But Dostoevsky believed in his characters. Mr Nabokov no longer believes in his, nor indeed in the novelist's art. He is open about his borrowing of Dostoevskyan techniques; at the same time he mocks them; he presents them, in the narrative itself, as indispensable but outdated clichés:

> Did it actually go on like this? . . . There is
> something a shade too literary about that talk
> of ours, smacking of thumb-screw conversations
> in those stage taverns where Dostoevski is at
> home; a little more of it and we should hear that

sibilant whisper of false humility, that catch in the breath, those repetitions of incantatory adverbs—and then all the rest of it would come, the mystical trimming dear to that famous writer of Russian thrillers.[1]

As is the case everywhere else, we must, in the novel, distinguish between a time for making tools and a time for reflecting on the tools made. Mr Nabokov is an author of the second period. He locates himself resolutely on the level of reflection. He never writes without *seeing himself* write, the way others hear themselves speak, and what interests him almost solely are the subtle deceptions of his reflective consciousness:

> I noticed that I was not thinking at all of what I thought I was thinking; attempted to catch my consciousness tripping, but got mazed myself.[2]

This passage, which subtly depicts the slide from wakefulness to sleep, shows up rather clearly the principal concern of the hero and the author of *Despair*. A rather curious work ensues, a novel of self-criticism and a self-criticism of the novel. It is reminiscent of Gide's *The Counterfeiters*. But in Gide's work the critic was also an experimenter: he tried out new techniques to see

---

1 Vladimir Nabokov, *Despair* (New York: Perigee Books, 1979), p. 98.

2 Nabokov, *Despair*, p. 106.

what results they would produce. Mr Nabokov (whether out of timidity or scepticism is not clear) is at pains not to invent a new technique. He mocks the artifices of the classical novel, but ends up using them himself, even if it means suddenly foreshortening a description or a piece of dialogue by writing, more or less, 'I'm stopping now, so as not to lapse into cliché.' This is all well and good, but what is the outcome? First a sense of unease. Closing the book, one thinks what a lot of fuss over nothing. And then, if Mr Nabokov is so superior to the novels he writes, why does he write them? You would swear it was out of masochism, so as to have the pleasure of catching himself red-handed in an act of fakery. And then, lastly, I'm willing to admit that Mr Nabokov is right to skip the big novelistic set-pieces, but what does he give us in their place? Preparatory chatter (though when we are duly readied, nothing happens), excellent little scenes, charming portraits and literary essays. Where is the novel? It has dissolved into its own venom: this is what I call a literature of the learned. The hero of *Despair* confesses: 'From the end of 1914 to the middle of 1919 I read exactly one thousand and eighteen books.'[3] I fear that Mr Nabokov, like his hero, has read too much.

But I can see another similarity too between the author and his character: both are victims of war and emigration. Admittedly, Dostoevsky has no shortage of cynical descendants today, with less stamina, but more

---

3 Nabokov, *Despair*, p. 14.

intelligence than their famous forebear. I have in mind, particularly, the Soviet writer Yuri Olesha. Only, for all Olesha's sly individualism, he is still part of Soviet society. He has roots. But at the present moment there is a curious literature of Russian—and other—émigrés, who are rootless. Mr Nabokov's rootlessness, like that of Hermann Karlovich is total. Neither is concerned with any society, even to rebel against it, because they belong to no society. As a result, Karlovich is reduced to committing perfect crimes and Mr Nabokov to writing, in the English language, on gratuitous themes.

1939

ON *THE SOUND AND THE FURY*:
TEMPORALITY IN FAULKNER

When you read *The Sound and the Fury*, what strikes you first are oddities of technique. Why has Faulkner broken up the timeline of his story and scrambled the pieces? Why is the first window that opens on to this fictional world the mind of an idiot? The reader is tempted to search out markers and re-establish the chronology for himself: 'Jason and Caroline Compson have had three sons and a daughter. The daughter, Caddy, has given herself to Dalton Ames and become pregnant by him. Forced to get hold of a husband quickly . . .' Here the reader stops, for he realizes that he is telling a different story. Faulkner didn't first conceive this orderly plot, then shuffle it like a pack of cards; he couldn't tell the story any other way. In the classical novel, there is a crux to the action: the murder of old Karamzov or the meeting of Édouard and Bernard in Gide's *The Counter-feiters*. One would look in vain for such a crux in *The Sound and the Fury*. Is it the castration of Benjy, Caddy's wretched amorous adventure, Quentin's suicide or Jason's hatred for his niece? Each episode, as soon as you look at it, opens up and reveals other episodes behind it—all the other episodes. Nothing happens; the story doesn't unfold: you discover it beneath every word, like a cumbrous, obscene presence, more or less condensed in each case. It would be wrong to regard these anomalies as gratuitous shows of virtuosity: a novelistic technique always relates to the novelist's metaphysics. The critic's task is to identify the latter before evaluating the former. It is blindingly obvious that Faulkner's metaphysics is a metaphysics of time.

It is man's misfortune that he is a temporal being. 'A man is the sum of his misfortunes. One day you'd think misfortune would get tired, but then time is your misfortune . . .'[4] This is the real subject of the novel. And if the technique Faulkner adopts seems at first a negation of temporality, this is because we are confusing temporality with chronology. It is man who invented dates and clocks: 'Constant speculation regarding the position of mechanical hands on an arbitrary dial which is a symptom of mind-function. Excrement Father said like

---

4 William Faulkner, *The Sound and the Fury*. Norton Critical Edition, 2nd edn (New York: W. W. Norton, 1994), p. 66.

sweating.'[5] To arrive at real time, we have to abandon this invented measure which in fact measures nothing: '. . . time is dead as long as it is being clicked off by little wheels; only when the clock stops does time come to life.'[6]

Quentin's act of smashing his watch thus has symbolic value: it takes us into clock-less time. And Benjy's time, too, is clock-less, he, the idiot, not knowing how to tell the time.

What is revealed at that point is the present. Not the ideal limit whose place is carefully marked between past and future. Faulkner's present is catastrophic in its essence. It is the event that comes upon us like a thief, enormous and unthinkable. That comes upon us and then disappears. Beyond that present, there is nothing, since the future doesn't exist. The present wells up from we know not where, chasing away another present. It is perpetually beginning anew: 'And . . . and . . . and then . . .' Like Dos Passos, but much more discreetly, Faulkner turns his narrative into an addition. The actions themselves, even when they are seen by those who perform them, break up and scatter as they penetrate into the present:

> I went to the dresser and took up the watch with the face still down. I tapped the crystal on

5 Faulkner, *The Sound and the Fury*, p. 49.

6 Faulkner, *The Sound and the Fury*, p. 54.

the dresser and caught the fragments of glass in my hand and put them into the ashtray and twisted the hands off and put them in the tray. The watch ticked on.[7]

The other characteristic of this present is a *sinking-down*. I use this word, for want of a better one, to point up a kind of motionless movement of this formless monster. There is never any progression in Faulkner, never anything that comes from the future. The present was not first a future possibility, as, for example, when my friend eventually appears, after having been *the man I am waiting for*. No, to be present means to appear without reason and to sink down. This sinking-down isn't part of some abstract vision: it is in things themselves that Faulkner perceives it and attempts to make his readers feel it:

> The train swung around the curve, the engine puffing with short, heavy blasts, and they passed smoothly from sight that way, with that quality of shabby and timeless patience, of static serenity . . .[8]

Or again,

> Beneath the sag of the buggy the hooves neatly rapid like motions of a lady doing embroidery,

---

7 Faulkner, *The Sound and the Fury*, p. 51.

8 Faulkner, *The Sound and the Fury*, p. 56.

diminishing without progress like a figure on a treadmill being drawn rapidly off-stage.[9]

It seems as though, in the very heart of things, Faulkner grasps a frozen speed: congealed spurting presences brush up against him that grow pale, retreat and reduce without moving.

Yet this elusive, unthinkable immobility can be halted and conceived of. Quentin can say, 'I broke my watch.' Only, when he says it, his act is already past. The past can be named and narrated; it can, to an extent, be grasped in concepts or recognized by the heart. We have already noted, writing of *Sartoris*, that Faulkner always showed events when they were finished. In *The Sound and the Fury*, everything happens in the wings: nothing happens, everything has happened. This is what enables us to understand the strange expression uttered by one of his heroes: 'I was, I am not.'[10] In this sense, too, Faulkner is able to make man a sum total without a future. He is 'the sum of his climatic experiences', 'the sum of his misfortunes', 'the sum of what have you': at every moment a line is drawn under events, since the present is merely a lawless rumbling, a past future. It seems Faulkner's worldview can be compared to that of a man sitting in an open-topped car and looking backwards. At each moment, formless shadows rear up to

---

9 The italics are Faulkner's.

10 Faulkner, *The Sound and the Fury*, p. 110.

right and left; flickerings, subdued vibrations, wisps of light, which only become trees, people and cars a little later, as they recede into the distance. The past acquires a sort of surreality in this: its outlines become crisp and hard—changeless. The present, nameless and fleeting, suffers greatly by comparison; it is full of holes and, through these holes, it is invaded by things past, which are fixed, still and silent, like judges or stares. Faulkner's monologues are reminiscent of aeroplane journeys with lots of air pockets. With each new pocket, the hero's consciousness sinks back into the past, rises and then sinks again. The present *is* not; it *becomes*; everything *was*. In *Sartoris*, the past was called 'stories', because these were—constructed—family memories and because Faulkner hadn't found his technique yet. In *The Sound and the Fury*, it is more individual and more undecided. But it is so obsessively there that at times it masks the present. And the present makes its way in the shadows like an underground river, reappearing only when it is, itself, past. When Quentin insults Bland,[11] he doesn't even realize he has done so: he is re-living his dispute with Dalton Ames. And when Bland beats him up, the brawl is overlaid with the one between Quentin and Ames. Later, Shreve *will relate* how Bland struck Quentin: he will relate the scene because it has now

---

11 Faulkner, *The Sound and the Fury*, pp. 100–04. See p. 102, the dialogue with Bland inserted into the dialogue with Ames, 'Did you ever have a sister, did you?' etc., and the inextricable confusion of the two battles.

become history, but when it was happening in the present, it was merely a veiled, furtive drift of events.

I was told once of a former deputy headmaster who had grown senile and whose memory had stopped like a broken watch: it now stood perpetually at the age of forty. He was sixty years old, but didn't know it and his last memory was of a school playground and the way he used to patrol its covered area each day. As a consequence, he interpreted his present in the light of this final stage of the past and walked round and round his table, convinced he was supervising schoolchildren at play. Faulkner's characters are like this. Worse: their past, though in order, isn't chronologically ordered. It is grouped into affective constellations. Around a number of central themes (Caddy's pregnancy, Benjy's castration and Quentin's suicide), innumerable silent clumps of memories gravitate. Hence the absurdity of chronology, of 'the assertive and contradictory assurance' of watchfaces:[12] the order of the past is the order of the heart. We shouldn't believe that the present, as it passes, becomes our closest memory. Its metamorphosis may sink it to the bottom of our memories, just as it may also leave it on the surface: only its own density and the overall dramatic meaning of our lives determine its level.

* * *

12 Faulkner, *The Sound and the Fury*, p. 54.

Such is Faulkner's time. And is it not familiar? This ineffable present, shipping water on all sides, these sudden invasions by the past, this affective order that stands opposed to the order of the intellect and the will (which is chronological, but misses reality), these memories, monstrous, intermittent obsessions, these waverings of the heart—is this not the lost—and regained—time of Marcel Proust? I am not unaware of the differences. I know, for example, that salvation, for Proust, lies in time itself, in the reappearance of the past as something whole and entire. For Faulkner, by contrast, the past is never lost—unfortunately. It is always there, an obsession. Only by mystic ecstasies can one escape the temporal world. A mystic is always a man who wants to forget something: his self or, more generally, language or figural representations. For Faulkner, it is time that has to be forgotten:

> Quentin, I give you the mausoleum of all hope and desire; it's rather excruciatingly apt that you will use it to gain the reductio ad absurdum of all human experience which can fit your individual needs no better than it fitted his or his father's. I give it to you not that you may remember time, *but that you might forget it now and then for a moment* and not spend all your breath trying to conquer it. Because no battle is ever won he said. They are not even fought. The field only reveals to man his own

folly and despair, and victory is an illusion of philosophers and fools.[13]

It is because he has forgotten time that the hunted negro of *Light in August* suddenly achieves his strange, dreadful happiness:

> It's not when you realize that nothing can help you—religion, pride, anything—it's when you realize that you don't need any aid.[14]

But for Faulkner, as for Proust, time is above all *what separates*. We remember the astonishment of the Proustian heroes who can no longer return to their past loves, of those lovers depicted in *Les Plaisirs et les Jours*, clinging to their passions because they are afraid they may pass and know that they will. We find the same anxiety in Faulkner:

> [P]eople cannot do anything that dreadful they cannot do anything very dreadful at all, they cannot even remember tomorrow what seemed dreadful today . . .[15]

and

> [A] love or sorrow is a bond purchased without design and which matures willy-nilly and is

---

13 Faulkner, *The Sound and the Fury*, p. 48.

14 Faulkner, *The Sound and the Fury*, p. 51.

15 Faulkner, *The Sound and the Fury*, p. 51.

recalled without warning to be replaced by whatever issue the gods happen to be floating at the time.[16]

In truth, Proust's novelistic technique *ought to have* been Faulkner's: it was the logical outcome of his metaphysics. But Faulkner is a lost man and it is because he feels lost that he takes risks, that he carries his thoughts through to their conclusions. Proust is a classicist and a Frenchman. The French lose themselves in a small-time sort of way and always end up finding themselves again. Eloquence, a taste for clear ideas and intellectualism caused Proust to maintain at least the semblance of chronology.

The deep causes of the affinity between the two are to be sought in a very general literary phenomenon: most great contemporary authors—Proust, Joyce, Dos Passos, Faulkner, Gide and Virginia Woolf—have, each in their own way, attempted to mutilate time. Some have shorn it of a past and future and reduced it to the pure intuition of the moment. Others, like Dos Passos, make it a dead, closed memory. Proust and Faulkner simply decapitated it. They took away its future: that is to say, the dimension of acts and freedom. Proust's heroes never undertake anything. Admittedly, they make plans, but their plans remain stuck to them alone; they cannot be thrown beyond the present, as bridges. They are dreams

---

16 Faulkner, *The Sound and the Fury*, pp. 112–13.

that reality puts to flight. The Albertine who appears isn't the one we were expecting, and the expectation is a mere inconsequential agitation, confined entirely to the present moment. As for Faulkner's heroes, they never see ahead; the car carries them off, facing backwards. The future suicide that throws its dense shadow over Quentin's last day isn't a human possibility: not for a second does Quentin consider that he might *not* kill himself. That suicide is an immobile wall, a *thing* Quentin approaches backwards, which he neither wants nor is able to conceive of: 'You seem to regard it merely as an experience that will whiten your hair overnight so to speak without altering your appearance at all.'[17] It isn't an *undertaking*, but a fateful inevitability. By losing its character as possibility, it ceases to exist in the future. It is already present, and Faulkner's whole art is directed at suggesting to us that Quentin's monologues and his last walk *were already* Quentin's suicide. It is in this way, I think, that the following curious paradox is explained: Quentin thinks his last day in the past tense, like someone remembering. But who is doing the remembering, since the hero's last thoughts coincide more or less with the shattering of his memory and his annihilation? The answer has to be that the novelist's skill lies in the choice of the present from which he narrates the past. And the present Faulkner has chosen here is the infinitesimal moment of death, as Salacrou does in *L'Inconnue*

---

17 Faulkner, *The Sound and the Fury*, p. 112.

d'Arras.[18] So, when Quentin's memory begins to unfurl his recollections ('Through the wall I heard Shreve's bed-springs and then his slippers on the floor hishing. I got up . . .'[19]), *he is already dead*. All this art and, to tell the truth, all this dishonesty are aimed simply at replacing the intuition of the future which the author lacks. Everything is then explained, beginning with the irrationality of time: since the present is the unexpected, the formless, it can acquire determinacy only by an overload of memories. We can understand, too, why *la durée* is 'man's characteristic misfortune': if the future has a reality, time distances us from the past and *brings us nearer* to the future; but if you abolish the future, time is now merely that which separates the present—which cuts it off—from itself. 'You cannot bear to think that someday it will no longer hurt you like this.' Man spends his time battling against time and it gnaws away at him like an acid, wrenches him away from himself and prevents him from fulfilling his humanity. Everything is absurd: 'Life is a tale told by an idiot, full of sound and fury, signifying nothing.'[20]

But does human time have no future? I can see that, for a nail or a clod of earth, time is a perpetual present. But is man merely a thinking nail? If we begin by plunging

---

18 Armand Salacrou (1899–1989): a French playwright, who is remembered particularly for *L'Inconnue d'Arras* of 1935. [Trans.]

19 Faulkner, *The Sound and The Fury*, p. 49.

20 William Shakespeare, *Macbeth*, Act V, Scene 5.

him into universal time, the time of nebulae and planets, of tertiary flexures and animal species, as into a bath of sulphuric acid, then that is the case. But a consciousness buffeted about in that way from one moment to another would have to be a consciousness *first* and only *thereafter* something temporal. Do we really believe that time can come to it from outside? Consciousness can 'be in time' only on condition that it becomes time in the very movement that makes it consciousness; it must, as Heidegger says, temporalize itself.[21] Man can no longer be arrested at each present and defined as 'the sum of what he has': the nature of consciousness implies, rather, that, of itself, it projects itself forward, towards the future; we can understand what it is only by what it will be and it is determined in its current being by its own possibilities. This is what Heidegger calls, 'the silent force of the possible'.[22] Faulkner's man, a creature deprived of possibilities, explained solely by what he was, is a being you will not recognize within yourself. Try to seize hold of your consciousness. Probe into it. You will see that it is hollow. You will find in it only futurity. I am not even speaking of your plans and expectations. But the very action you catch in passing has meaning for you only if you can project its completion outside of itself, outside of you, into the 'not yet'. This very cup with its bottom

21 The reference is presumably to Heidegger's use of the term (*sich*) *zeitigen*. [Trans.]

22 '*Die stille Kraft des Möglichen*'. [Trans.]

that you do not see—that you could see and that is at the end of a movement you have not yet made—this white sheet of paper, the underside of which is hidden (but you could turn it over) and all the stable, bulky objects surrounding us display their most immediate, most solid qualities in the future. Man is in no sense the sum total of what he has, but the totality of what he doesn't yet have, of what he could have. And if we are immersed, in this way, in futurity, isn't the formless harshness of the present thereby attenuated? The event doesn't spring on us like a thief, since it is, by its very nature, a Having-been-Future. And, in seeking to explain the past, isn't it first the historian's task to research into its future? I rather suspect that the absurdity Faulkner finds in a human life is an absurdity he first put there himself. Not that human life isn't absurd: but there is another form of absurdity.

How does it come about that Faulkner and so many other authors chose that particular absurdity, which is so un-novelistic and so untrue? I believe we have to look for the cause in the social conditions of our present life. Faulkner's despair seems to me to antedate his metaphysics. For him, as for all of us, the future is blocked off. Everything we see and experience suggests to us that 'this cannot last', and yet change is not even conceivable, except in cataclysmic form. We are living in an age of impossible revolutions and Faulkner employs his extraordinary art to describe this world that is dying of old age and our suffocation in it. I love his art; I do not believe in his metaphysics. A blocked-off future is still a future. 'Even when human reality still exists but has nothing more "before it" and has "settled [*abgeschlossen*] its account", its Being is still determined by the "ahead-of-itself". Hopelessness, for example, doesn't tear human reality away from its possibilities, but is only one of its own modes of *Being-towards* these possibilities.'[23]

23 Martin Heidegger, *Being and Time* (John Macquarrie and Edward Robinson trans.) (Oxford: Basil Blackwell, 1978), p. 279. Translation modified to reflect Sartre's rendering of Dasein as '*la réalité humaine*'. [Trans.]

✳

A NOTE ON SOURCES

'*Sartoris* by William Faulkner'

Originally published as '*Sartoris* par W. Faulkner' in *Situations I* (Paris: Gallimard, 1947), pp. 7–13.

First published in English translation in *Critical Essays* (London: Seagull Books, 2010), pp. 1–12.

'On John Dos Passos and *1919*'

Originally published as 'A propos de John dos Passos et de *1919*' in *Situations I* (Paris: Gallimard, 1947), pp. 14–24.

First published in English translation in *Critical Essays* (London: Seagull Books, 2010), pp. 13–31.

'*Despair* by Vladimir Nabokov'

Originally published as 'Vladimir Nabokov: *La Méprise*' in *Situations I* (Paris: Gallimard, 1947), pp. 53–6.

First published in English translation in *Critical Essays* (London: Seagull Books, 2010), pp. 85–90.

'On *The Sound and the Fury*: Temporality in Faulkner'

Originally published as 'A propos de *Le Bruit et la Fureur*. La temporalité chez Faulkner' in *Situations I* (Paris: Gallimard, 1947), pp. 65–75.

First published in English translation in *Critical Essays* (London: Seagull Books, 2010), pp. 104–21.